BERLIN

CITY GUIDE *for* DESIGN LOVERS

The Travel Colours City Guides are for design-loving travellers who like to explore the trendiest places in each city, for travellers who see themselves as trendsetters. Each City Guide features a curated selection of the best places to "sleep, eat, drink, shop and explore", all of which have been personally tried and tested.

Edition TWO

EDITOR IN CHIEF
STEFANIE FRIESE

WORDS BY
HANNI HEINRICH

PHOTOGRAPHY BY
CAITLIN COLLINS

PUBLISHED BY
FRIESE MEDIA GMBH, 2020
2ND EDITION - MARCH 2020

PRINTED AND BOUND BY
HARTMANNDRUCK & MEDIEN GMBH IN
GERMANY ON FSC CERTIFIED UNCOATED
PAPER

ISBN   978-3-9821148-8-0

SAY HELLO

GENERAL ENQUIRIES: hello@travelcolours.de
DISTRIBUTION: sales@travelcolours.de

GET THE BOOKS ONLINE AT
www.travelcolours.guide

WE TAKE CARE

OF YOU AND OF MOTHER EARTH

We work closely with a family-run printing company that has been printing climate-neutral for years together with ClimatePartner. All our books are printed exclusively on FSC-certified paper.

STEFANIE FRIESE
FOUNDER & EDITOR IN CHIEF

It has to be nice and a bit different. The desire for lifestyle and design is always guaranteed. As the founder of Travel Colours, Stefanie is always in search of the most beautiful places.

HANNI HEINRICH
EDITOR

As a writer, Hanni is inspired by people, human behaviour and beaches. Her favourite body lotion is sun blocker factor 50. Born in Merseburg, Germany, she is currently based in Cape Town.

CAITLIN COLLINS
PHOTOGRAPHER

Texan expat Caitlin Collins finds the German winters bitterly cold, yet she always has that sparkle that becharms everyone in close vicinity to her.

LOVE LETTER

Following the fall of the Wall, Berlin quickly emerged as one of the most cosmopolitan, creative and exciting cities in Europe for art, museums, architecture, history, and nightlife. From exhibitions and events, openings and vernissages to open-air festivals – there is always something happening in this city. While Berlin has always attracted visitors to its nightlife and modern art scene, the past six years have seen much movement in Berlin's booming food scene. Today, high-quality fusion kitchens with influences from all over the world abound in Berlin. New restaurants, rival gallery openings, and local produce is high design. Berlin is the birthplace of new German cuisine and the place in Germany where food trends first start. With a countless number of bars, restaurants and cafés to choose from, this Berlin Guide will show you a curated selection of our favourite places to "sleep, eat, drink, shop and explore". From cosy cafés and coffee roasteries to restaurants with menus boasting products from local artisans and growers, and Berlin's most prestigious fashion shops hidden in a backyard, this guide will lead you away from the tourist hubs to some of Berlin's hidden local gems.

Stefanie Friese

EDITOR IN CHIEF

SLEEP

GORKI APARTMENTS

INDIVIDUALLY DESIGNED SPACES

Located in Berlin Mitte, the Gorki Apartments combine the style and hospitality of a comfortable boutique hotel with privacy. Here, guests don't have to worry about anything: Gorki Apartments offer an effortless living experience. The staff know what it takes to make each apartment feel like home. The Gorki Apartments are full of discoveries and creative flair, thanks to the building's original patina, which has been updated for modern living. Each of the theatrically proportioned apartments provides the perfect retreat to kick back and relax after a day (or night) in town. Each room radiates subtle aromas of lime, linden blossoms, herbaceous honey and fresh green foliage to ensure one never forgets a stay. This disarmingly nonchalant summer scent is made by Frau Tonis Parfum Berlin.

Weinbergsweg 25, 10119 Berlin
www.gorkiapartments.com

SOHO HOUSE BERLIN

PRIVATE MEMBERS' CLUB

Plush sofas, vintage bar stools, fireside seating and contemporary art: Soho House Berlin is a stylish world, offering luxury interiors and premium drinking and dining. The Soho House Berlin is a private members' club and hotel in a memorial-proof building located in Mitte. Close to Alexanderplatz, it is conveniently central and an ideal space to work, meet and relax. The heated pool on the rooftop is 26°C all-year-round. Soho House boasts 65 bedrooms, 20 apartments and four spacious lofts, which come in various sizes. There are different luxury amenities, depending on the size and type of room. Each room, however, features Egyptian cotton sheets and exclusive access to the club floor, gym and rooftop pool.

Torstraße 1, 10119 Berlin
www.sohohouseberlin.com

SO/ BERLIN DAS STUE

LUXURY BOUTIQUE HOTEL

This luxury boutique hotel offers bold design and Berliner locality and was built in the late 1930s by KaDeWe architect Johann Emil Schaudt. SO/ Berlin Das Stue is located in the heart of Berlin's embassy district – near the Landwehr Canal in the immediate vicinity of Berlin Zoo. Here the view over the Tiergarten, the zoo, and Berlin's western and eastern skyline is unrestricted. It allows guests to relax in the heart of the bustling capital. With the five-metre-high ceilings, free-standing bathtubs and exclusive materials, the hotel suites have the flair of spacious city villas. Some of the rooms have a balcony or terrace and many of them have floor-to-ceiling windows. SO/ Berlin Das Stue is also famous for its exquisite wine collection with award-winning wines from Germany, Spain and Austria.

Drakestraße 1, 10787 Berlin
www.das-stue.com

AMO BY AMANO

URBAN LIVING FEELING

Hotel AMO by AMANO is a true Berlin original with an extraordinary look. The typical Berlin building combines a characteristic cityscape with modern architecture. Here the unexpected arises: the hotel reception is located underground and is familiarly welcoming. There is also the AMO bar in the basement that serves sophisticated cocktails in an exuberant atmosphere and the in-house restaurant, JOSEPH, on the ground floor offering delectable Israeli cuisine. The 93 rooms offer a quiet retreat and stylish cosiness. Just outside the front door, the heart of the city beats as Hotel AMO is centrally located in Mitte, right at the Oranienburger Tor. This hotel promises excitement, whether one is above ground or below.

Friedrichstraße 113, 10117 Berlin
www.amanogroup.de/de/hotels/amo

HOTEL ZOO

THE CLASH OF HISTORY AND MODERN AGE

If the walls of the Hotel Zoo Berlin could speak, they would tell stories of stars, boom and decadence, destruction and reconstruction. Built in 1889 as a private residence, the building's legacy as a hotel began in 1911. Located in the heart of City West, in the middle of the famous Kurfürstendamm, the crème de la crème of intellectuals, artists, personalities, and managers reside at this prestigious hotel. Today, it is still popular during celebrity events, whether it is Berlinale or Fashion Week. The historical character has been preserved with thoughtful attention to detail and original elements. The modern elements are New Yorker flair infused with London townhouse elegance. The spacious rooms and suites are equally eccentric featuring bespoke furniture and typical Berliner spirit.

Kurfürstendamm 25, 10719 Berlin
www.hotelzoo.de

SIR SAVIGNY

DESIGN HOTEL WITH A CREATIVE SPIRIT

This is not a usual hotel. This is a home. And a playground. Sir Savigny offers every possibility imaginable. From fast bikes, yoga retreats and clubbing to a Berliner beer tasting and a graffiti-culture tour to migrant history. It offers the most authentic activities with the most authentic Berliners. Sir Savigny is small and stylish. This hotel deliberately refrains from having a reception desk: guests step directly into an area full of books and a fireplace, and check-in and check-out is explained on the couch. With only 44 rooms, Sir Savigny is an oasis where one can find quietness in the middle of Berlin. Savigny's motto is: take a pause, enjoy the fragrant orange trees in the backyard, okay, maybe connect to the Wi-Fi, but in any case, enjoy the time in Berlin (and a tasty burger at the in-house bar, The Butcher).

Kantstraße 144, 10623 Berlin
www.sirhotels.com/de/savigny

MICHELBERGER HOTEL

CREATIVE, UNIQUE, AND PERSONAL

Located near the East Side Gallery, this hotel is close to the Friedrichshain's infamous nightlife. The Michelberger is offering a range of funky rooms, a buzzy bar and a courtyard for guests to relax, work, eat, listen to music and catch up with friends. Designed by the hotel's in-house design team along with many other renowned designers, the Michelberger oozes difference. GDR-inspired chandeliers made from thick, handblown glass hang from the ceiling; low lying sofas made from a solid timber base, with upholstered cushions invite one to relax. Friendly staff make every guest feel at home. Seven different room categories present distinct styles and functions – from cosy love nests to luxury rooms – with plenty of built-in wooden components.

Warschauer Str. 39-40, 10243 Berlin
www.michelbergerhotel.com

PROVOCATEUR HOTEL

GLAMOROUS. DECADENT. PLAYFUL.

This hotel is pretty. It is also delightful and extremely tempting. Located at the Brandenburgische Strasse, within walking distance of Kurfürstendamm, it offers a great location from which to discover the western part of the city. Sightseeing spots and green parks are close by too. The Provocateur is glamorous and reminds one of a naughty night in 1920s Paris and at the same time reflects the heartbeat of modern Berlin. At the restaurant, Chef Duc Ngo seduces guests with his otherworldly French-Chinese culinary creations and the hotel bar envelops guests with its seductive atmosphere, enchanting elixirs, and intoxicating music and dance. Whether sleeping, living or celebrating – the Provocateur seduces everyone with its extraordinary flair.

Brandenburgische Str. 21, 10707 Berlin
www.provocateur-hotel.com

EAT

WITH COFFEE

BETTY'N CATY

VIBRANT NEIGHBORHOOD CAFÉ

Named after the owners, this lovely cafe is located in Berlin's famous Prenzlauer Berg. Besides big and small breakfasts until 5.30pm, the menu also offers acai bowls and power muesli or porridge with winter spices. The list of salad choices is equally as long. Organic egg dishes, as well as hearty meals are also available. Not only is the food tasty and good looking, but also the cafe itself. A dark wooden floor with white Parisian metro tiles and the zinc-topped bar lets Betty'n Caty shine in this area. The wooden chairs and tables have been specially made and the benches covered with blue velvet invite everyone to linger. A reservation is highly recommended.

Knaackstraße 26, 10405 Berlin
www.bettyncaty.com

ALBATROSS

FRESHLY-BAKED PASTRIES & BREAD

Albatross is a small bakery and cafe located in Kreuzberg offering homemade sourdough breads and buns, Viennoiserie pastries, patisseries and cakes as well as lunch options. Anyone who has tried the cinnamon rolls or sourdough bread has fallen in love at the first bite. It is a shining star in Berlin's bread-heaven. Besides, Albatross aims to be a diverse workplace where everybody feels safe, welcome and appreciated. This Kreuzberg bakery works with a high degree of responsibility and transparency, uses locally-sourced ingredients and supplies over 50 cafés and restaurants, including The Store at Soho House and Distrikt Coffee in Mitte. The walls are bare and partly exposed. The real eye-catcher is the counter, which every customer walks straight into when entering the bakery.

Graefestraße 66/67, 10967 Berlin
www.instagram.com/albatrossberlin

BALDON

PLATFORM FOR CREATIVE EXPERIENCES

Baldon is a canteen, restaurant and bar located in the LOBE BLOCK, a brutalist concrete building in the wedding district. Built by architects Arno Brandlhuber and Muck Petzet, the building offers space for studios, agencies, a yoga studio – and for Baldon. Founders Jessica-Joyce Sidon and Caecilia Baldszus serve lunch with a vegetarian focus on weekdays and coffee is available any time of the day. Ingredients, and most of the interior decor, are locally sourced. Artworks by Peter Klare decorate the towering walls. And those who cannot get enough of Baldon can participate in various workshops and events taking place here.

Böttgerstraße 16, 13357 Berlin
www.baldon.berlin

HALLMANN & KLEE

CHIC BISTRO RESTAURANT

This elegant and chic bistro restaurant is located in Berlin's hip Neukölln area. Carefully-selected suppliers and organic ingredients combined with extraordinary service and comfortable interior design ensure a magical experience for all the senses. Major emphasis is placed on the traditional preparation of all dishes. Here, handmade truly means made by hand and homemade. This restaurant is faintly reminiscent of a garden as herbs are grown in the kitchen. Every Friday, homemade jams, chocolates and olive oil are on sale. Hallmann & Klee practises holistic sustainability and inspires its guests.

Böhmische Str. 13, 12055 Berlin
www.hallmann-klee.de

KANTINE

LUNCH DATE WITH ARCHITECTS

This bistro offers simple European but tasty food from a short daily menu. Chipperfield Kantine is set in David Chipperfield Architects' office. The sleek minimalist interior design gives off super cool vibes, yet it is cosy and vibey. If one ever wants to have a lunch date with architects, then visit Chipperfields. It is not only the architecture that is tasteful. At this canteen, the lunch menu, which changes daily, contains delicious items such as the classic German dish Senfeier (boiled eggs in a mustard sauce) with spinach and mashed potatoes, or beef stroganoff with pasta, a salad with radishes and goat cheese, or an organic chicken leg with green beans and potato salad, all impeccably served.

Joachimstraße 11, 10119 Berlin
www.kantine-berlinmitte.de

HALLESCHES HAUS

GENERAL STORE, LUNCHROOM & EVENT SPACE

Berlin knows how to combine a modern lunchtime restaurant with a contemporary concept store including stylish furnishings and a green outdoor area. The personification of this is Hallesches Haus located near the Hallesches Tor in the Kreuzberg district. Built in 1902, the former post office has transformed into a concept store offering a range of designer household products from small furniture, kitchen and bathroom accessories to garden appliances. Beauty, wellness and fashion products are also available. The daily breakfast and lunch menu offers healthy food sourced from local producers. Popular are dishes such as scrambled eggs on Sironi sourdough bread, Hokkaido squash salad with whipped tofu, and freshly baked cookies or carrot cake. Of course, the coffee is great too.

Tempelhofer Ufer 1, 10961 Berlin
www.hallescheshaus.com

KAFFEEBAR

HEALTHY EATING THAT TASTES GOOD

This Kreuzberg cafe caters for both early and late risers, opening at 7:30am and offering breakfast until 3pm. The creators behind are half German/half Australian and believe in healthy, sustainable eating. Coffee, cake, sweet treats, fresh juices and tasty brunch items are all homemade, with many gluten-free and vegan options available. The interior is practical with a hint of industrial. Wooden tables and sofas create a warm and cosy atmosphere inside. Tables out front allow one to enjoy a cup of coffee while refuelling in the sunlight in the warmer months. If one needs catering, the KAFFEEBAR team can offer their expertise, tailoring their service to accommodate virtually any dietary need.

Graefestraße 8, 10967 Berlin
www.kaffeebar-berlin.com

DISTRIKT COFFEE

ALL-DAY BRUNCH MENU

This is a hip coffeehouse in Mitte where one can also have an all-day breakfast and lunch. Popular choices include overnight oats with superfoods, avocado with yellow beets and eggs on sourdough toast and French toast with berries and creme fraiche. The sweet-toothed can choose between homemade cakes and pastries from the popular Kreuzberg bakery Albatross. The wooden and black steel tables and chairs are placed in front of raw brick walls while the chequered floor straddles the line between casual and elegant. Distrikt uses different beans from international and local coffee roasters such as Fjord Berlin, Coffee Collective and La Cabra, while its carefully curated tea selection comes from Companion Tea in Kreuzberg. Fresh homemade drinks are prepared daily.

Bergstraße 68, 10115 Berlin
www.distriktcoffee.de

SILO COFFEE

GREAT COFFEE, VIBRANT FOOD

This is a minimalist, stylish cafe with large wooden tables that serves more than avocado sandwiches and coffee. It is the prime coffee and breakfast spot in Friedrichshain, close to the Boxhagener Platz. The flat whites rank among the city's best. Sweet and savoury dishes, as well as juices, teas, homemade iced teas, lemonades and ginger shots, are available. The Silo signature: Organic poached eggs, oyster mushrooms, truffle, pecorino, herbs and lemon with sourdough toast. It's an explosion of flavour and intense colours. The overall simple, but practical interior creates a Scandinavian feel to this cafe. For hot summer days, there are also a couple of seats available on the sidewalk. Silo Coffee is also constantly innovating and organising events.

Gabriel-Max-Straße 4, 10245 Berlin
www.silo-coffee.com

BONANZA

WELL KNOWN ROASTERS

Bonanza serves coffee on a world-class level. It roasts as little as possible, but enough to fully develop all flavours – free from the tastes that are produced by the roast itself. Bonanza has two stores. The tiny cafe Bonanza Coffee Heroes is on Oderbergerstrasse, where people queue, especially on weekends, to get one of the best coffees in Berlin. The roastery on Adalbertstrasse in Kreuzberg is a spacious room, with elegant furniture. Here, they roast beans, organise tastings and manage a little shop. The bright space is divided into two parts by a huge glass-panelled wall, allowing customers to watch the staff roast, test and package the products.

Adalbertstraße 70, 10999 Berlin
www.bonanzacoffee.de

LE BON

BRUNCH. LUNCH. COCKTAILS.

Brunch. Lunch. Cocktails. A bit more sophisticated than anywhere else. Located between Kreuzberg and Neukölln in Kreuzkölln, Le Bon offers international brunch favourites as well as a weekly rotating lunch, especially popular among the Kiez locals. The restaurant's solid wooden tables and rough concrete floors represent the typical Berlin industrial look. Popular on the brunch menu are caramelised grapefruit, granola, pancakes, shakshuka and various egg dishes like the famous slow cooked "60 min egg" open sandwich. There are smoothies and fresh juices for a healthy start of the day and boozy brunch options.

Boppstraße 1, 10967 Berlin
www.lebon-berlin.com

SPINDLER

RELAXED BRASSERIE-RESTAURANT

SPINDLER is a relaxed brasserie on the banks of the Landwehr Canal in Kreuzberg. Whether for a business lunch, dinner, or a drink on the terrace, SPINDLER is open seven days a week from early till late. The building is over 100 years old and the renovated interior was decorated by designer Karolina Preis using handmade furniture and selected antiques. SPINDLER offers modern, regional cuisine with a French touch such as beetroot marinated Salmon with Ricotta and Roots, homemade Farmer Terrine or Pan-fried Duck Breast with Pommes Dauphine and Red Wine Jus. The kitchen crew creates classic dishes from regional, seasonal and homemade ingredients. In summer, all meals can be enjoyed outside on a romantic cast-iron bench, idly watching the river.

Paul-Lincke-Ufer 42/43, 10999 Berlin
www.spindler-berlin.de

DALUMA

NATURAL GOOD NUTRIENTS

This shop operates on a new level: better nutrition for the body, better taste for the mind, and higher sustainability for the world. Fruit and vegetables come from certified organic farms. Face masks, moisturisers and supplements contain natural ingredients and high-quality standards are a basic requirement for the preparation. Serving fair trade coffee from Columbia showing absolute transparency, Daluma also helps to build schools and supports sustainable farming methods and fair direct trade in Ethiopia. Daluma is certainly also a business enterprise, but here it is compulsory to promote sustainability and treat employees and partners fairly and on equal terms. With its flagship store in Charlottenburg and shops in Mitte and at the well-known KaDeWe, Daluma contributes towards a better world.

Schlüterstraße 38, 10629 Berlin
www.daluma.de

THE BARN

A LEADING COFFEE ROASTER

Berlin's coffee roasters are dedicated. The Barn sources, roasts and serves the highest quality. Through strong partnerships with sustainable coffee growers, The Barn provides access to prime lots of each harvest. Established as a meeting point for coffee lovers in Berlin Mitte since 2010, The Barn Roastery was added in 2012 with a second coffee roaster. Today, the Barn family has further institutions: the Cafe Kranzler, one of the oldest coffee houses in Berlin, and other cafes were opened in the wild district of Neukölln, the chic Hackescher Markt and the famous Potsdamer Platz. The coffee shop and the roaster made history and are now known beyond the borders of Berlin and Germany.

Schönhauser Allee 8, 10119 Berlin
www.thebarn.de

EAT

WITH WINE

PANAMA

SEASONAL PRODUCE AND EXOTIC SPICES

Crispy pig ear in oyster mayonnaise and empanadas, meat-filled dumplings with ponzu sauce. One thing is clear at Panama: your taste buds will go BOOM.

The menu is a take on contemporary German cuisine with experimental twists of South American flavours, a hint of Asia, a breeze across the continents. And, the excellent wine list reflects current trends. Panama is located in a backyard off Potsdamer Strasse, which has become one of Berlin's most prestigious areas. Fittingly, Panama's rooms are filled with the work of contemporary artists, many of them from friends of restaurant owner Cramer-Klett. The showpiece is a light sculpture made of vintage lights. Eating here, surrounded by the sea-green tiles, yellow seats and summery decor, is meant to be a journey.

Potsdamer Straße 91, 10785 Berlin

www.oh-panama.com

LODE & STIJN

CELEBRATING REGIONAL PRODUCTS

One principle counts: what's on the table will be eaten. End of discussion. At Lode & Stijn, the chef works on a culinary masterpiece that categorically excludes any change. The Dutch founders, Lode van Zuylen and Stijn Remi, source seasonal produce from regional suppliers and serve only a five-course menu. Each meal served in a casual, yet refined setting. Selected wine complements each course. Each dish has a clearly defined focus that is not bombarded with many flavours, and the foods appear natural without being boring. Only one dessert is available each day. Lode & Stijn is able to accommodate allergies and food sensitivities, and can also offer a vegetarian menu.

Lausitzer Str. 25, 10999 Berlin
www.lode-stijn.de

OTTO

PURELY NATURAL INGREDIENTS

Experimental, unconventional, regional: Vadim Otto Ursus' new restaurant located at Prenzlauer Berg joins the chain of innovative and alternative concepts in Berlin. Vadim's team focuses on using purely natural ingredients and using every little animal or vegetable component. Fermented vegetables, sauces prepared from boiled fish carcasses according to Japanese tradition, self-matured ham from local cows in Brandenburg. Many products come from neighbours and friends in the countryside. The idea behind otto's concept is to sensitise everyone to the environment, nature, the seasons and sustainable food. The dining room, which is surrounded by concrete walls, has an open kitchen and only holds 19 seats with woodwork by Mathias Swarowsky, which gives the cool look more intimacy.

Oderberger Str. 56, 10435 Berlin
www.ottoursus.de

CODA

BERLIN'S FIRST DESSERT RESTAURANT

This is Berlin's first dessert restaurant and another addition to the culinary scene in Neukölln. Coda is the perfect place to round off a day. It offers a sensual experience, a new cocktail culture and new experimental desserts. Coda is a unique fine-dining experience. No artificial flavours, no colours or other additives. Each dessert benefits from high-quality and fresh ingredients. Chef Rene Frank's style is based on the craft of modern pastry, mostly refraining from white flour, white sugar and fat. Coda gains sweetness from fruits and vegetables, as well as saltiness from ingredients such as anchovies or cheese, bitter substances from plants and herbs, acidity from citrus fruits or tamarind, umami from protein-rich foods. The interior is pure and clean, like all of the ingredients at Coda.

Friedelstraße 47, 12047 Berlin
www.coda-berlin.com

TISK SPEISEKNEIPE

SOPHISTICATED BERLIN CLASSICS

What better way to experience a pulsating neighbourhood than by eating and drinking together? In the middle of Neukölln, life and change pulsates between Kindl Areal, Dönerplaces and the Neukölln Town Hall. Here the TISK bar welcomes everyone. A menu with drink pairing is presented at the counter and dishes are served directly from the open kitchen. Alternatively, guests will be served refined a la carte dishes in the guest room. The kitchen focuses on Berlin classics in a new guise, based on regional products. Martin Müller, the owner, manager and chef stands behind this concept. The TISK Speisekneipe accommodates 50 people and with its fully-equipped bar invites everyone to live to the fullest – from an aperitif to a nightcap.

Neckarstraße 12, 12053 Berlin
www.tisk-speisekneipe.de

BARRA

SERVING SMALL SHARING PLATES

This restaurant serves high-quality dishes without many frills. Located at the Neuköllner Schillerkiez, Barra is a charming restaurant, serving small dishes for guests to share. It does rely on regional, high-quality products and the seasons dictate the daily menu, which changes according to what produce is available. British emigrants are making the magic here, for neighbours, for guests, and for everyone who likes to share a great meal. By the way, Barra derives from the old Gaelic word Barr, meaning crop or yield and referring to produce. Nevertheless, the focus here is on natural wine. The wooden interior is welcoming and the lamps cast beautiful light, exactly where one wants it to be.

Okerstraße 2, 12049 Berlin
www.barraberlin.com

CECCONI'S

MODERN, SOPHISTICATED ITALIAN

Cecconi's is an Italian restaurant characterised by urban zeitgeist and elegance. From Mondays to Saturdays it is open morning to evening and offers an a la carte menu. Ceconni's serves lunch and dinner from Monday to Saturday and brunch and dinner on Saturday and Sunday. Cecconi's specialises in homemade pasta, fish and dishes from Italy. Guests enter through the main entrance of The Soho House Berlin. The open kitchen, a wood-burning stove, the marble floor and red leather sofas radiate sophistication and warmth at the same time. This is a place to feel comfortable and at home in a very elegant way. During the summer months, guests can enjoy the open terrace.

Torstraße 1, 10119 Berlin
www.cecconisberlin.com

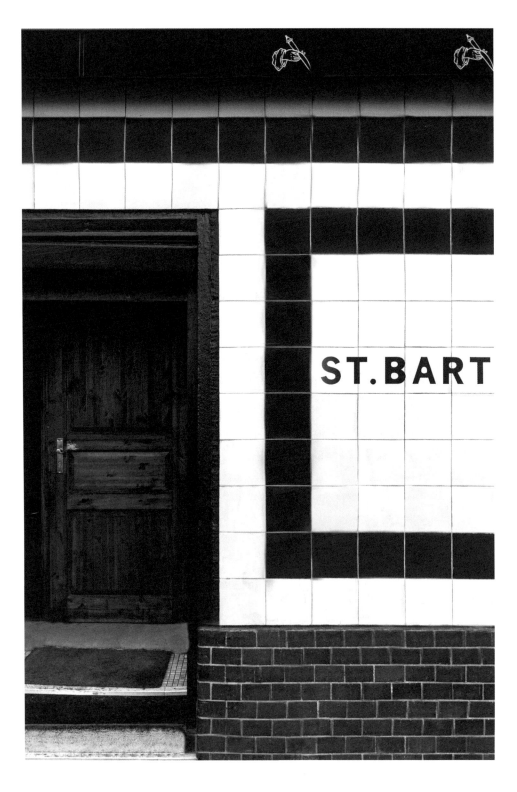

ST. BART

OLD-BERLIN-PUB AMBIENCE

The Kreuzberg restaurant St. Bart offers international specialties with wine, cocktail and beers. Modern cuisine is served in a typical old-Berlin-pub ambience, celebrating homely dark wood. St. Bart confidently presents itself as a gastro-pub and aims to remain down to earth among culinary fashion movements. Try the cockles with anchovy butter and fried Brandenburg Free Range chicken. St Bart's bread comes from the famous Albatross bakery. Nothing processed, everything natural, from nose-to-tail. Chef Lee Thompson offers small and large dishes, and also adds the occasional German touch, for example, the German blood pudding and potato dish Himmel & Erde. One is lucky to get a seat without a reservation, however, St. Bart welcomes bar walk-ins in any case.

Graefestraße 71, 10967 Berlin
www.stbartpub.com

893 RYŌTEI

FINE, JAPANESE CUISINE

Run by famous chef Duc Ngo, 893 Ryōtei is a clever city restaurant, a Japanese food bar with puristic design and no kitsch, dark in the room and bright at the bar seats. Ryōtei traditionally means classic Japanese restaurant, although this one leads one astray insofar as it is a contemporary food bar, where traditional Japanese recipes are combined with foreign ingredients. The hit at 893 Ryōtei is Tuna & Foie Gras, a tuna tartare with fries, fig jam and topped with foie gras. The crispy grilled octopus with small, peeled tomatoes, avocado cubes and sesame dressing, Yasai Yaki Udon in a very large bowl with plenty of pak choi and Japanese mushrooms are also among the most popular dishes. Duc Ngo has created a magnetic place.

Kantstraße 135, 10625 Berlin
www.893ryotei.de

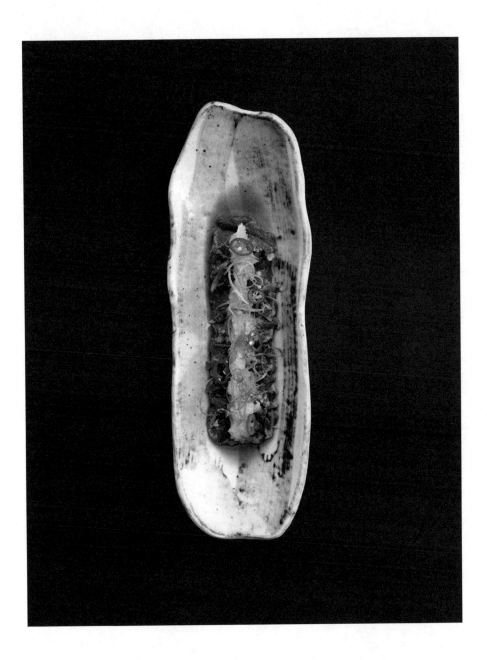

ERNST

12 SEAT RESTAURANT IN WEDDING

Ernst is an ambitious restaurant in Wedding. Only twelve guests can find seating at the L-shaped bar, booked out months in advance. Guests can see how about 30 servings are prepared in the open kitchen: Carrot swirled in raw milk butter and caramelised in its own juice. Grilled cucumber with apple cider vinegar jelly. Plenty a la minute and often only one ingredient on the plate. Ernst reflects the sensitivity of the seasons. The menu is changed daily with carefully selected ingredients from farms around the Brandenburg area. Dylan Watson-Brawn and Spencer Christenson, Canadian-born chefs and co-owners, together with sommelier Christoph Geyler celebrate absolutely every detail, no matter how small. No other German restaurant currently enjoys more international attention.

Gerichtstraße 54, 13347 Berlin
www.ernstberlin.de

LOKAL

DAILY-CHANGING MENU

Chic, elegant and minimalistic. White Shaker-style chairs, classic wooden tables and white walls radiate peace. Lokal is known for its daily-changing menu, fresh food and not-so-common dishes such as ox tongue, goose and chestnuts, or potato wedges and a pickle. Everything is homemade and delicious, of course, and the portions are very generous. The priority here is high-quality ingredients combined with good company and time. Time to indulge and savour local food over great conversation. The fanciness at Lokal lies in the innovative dishes, large portions and a good price. It's no surprise that this restaurant remains popular among the trendy Berlin crowd.

Linienstraße 160, 10115 Berlin
www.lokal-berlin.blogspot.de

FREA

VEGAN AND ZERO-WASTE

FREA is the first plant-based, vegan and zero-waste restaurant in Berlin Mitte, located on Torstrasse. All dishes are freshly prepared on-site and only selected organic ingredients are used. FREA produces as much as possible, for example, sourdough bread, hazelnut milk, kombucha and dark chocolate. The wooden interior is simple, yet elegant and emphasises the love of nature. Natural light floods the restaurant through the large windows, making the many indoor plants happy. True to its motto "full taste, zero waste", FREA processes food waste through composting and the composted soil substitute is returned to the suppliers. FREA is a place that combines indulgence with sustainability.

Torstraße 180, 10115 Berlin
www.frea.de

NIGHT KITCHEN

ATMOSPHERE OF TEL AVIV

In the Heckman Höfe in Mitte lies a popular spot for a night out, the Night Kitchen bar and restaurant. Packed almost every night with the vibrant Berlin crowd, reservations are highly recommended. Night Kitchen is a contemporary Mediterranean dining bar. As Gilad Heimann, the owner of Night Kitchen describes it: "A no-stress-no-fuss night out with friends sitting on the bar, eating good food and drinking throughout the night." All dishes are made with the best local ingredients and a modern twist and are meant to be shared. This 'Dinner with Friends' promises a journey through taste, where waiters host and guide through the night. The Night Kitchen concept brings the atmosphere of Tel Aviv into the heart of Berlin.

Heckmann Höfe, Oranienburger Str. 32, 10117 Berlin
www.nightkitchenberlin.com

TULUS LOTREK

RELAXED, YET TOP-CLASS RESTAURANT

Located in Berlin-Kreuzberg this place is considered to be a particularly relaxed, yet top-class restaurant. It welcomes customers with warm attentive service that fits its casual character. Good light, great wallpaper, comfortable seating in several rooms and lots of air in between the tables are the atmospheric basics that radiate cosiness. A slightly French breeze emanates from the kitchen: Chef Max Strohe is well known as a guest on Tim Mälzer's show Kitchen Impossible and also as the most relaxed Michelin-star chef in the country. Every single trace of taste can be smelt and tasted clearly on the spoon, and yet all of this is new on the palate. This restaurant is a mandatory address for urban hedonists.

Fichtestraße 24, 10967 Berlin
www.tuluslotrek.de

DRINK

DAS HOTEL

FEELING OF BEING IN LOVE

The feeling of being in love is best experienced at the Das Hotel, which is true to the Berlin-style simply called neo-romanticism. The heart piece of Das Hotel is the bar counter. It is mostly candlelit and characterised by an abundance of flowers. They hang from the ceiling, as if they were thrown into the air and then suspended frozen to be admired forever. The cocktails and long drinks are top quality and are made using in-house created essences. The atmosphere and spirit here is clearly international and seeks a connection to humanity. Das Hotel is a bar and perhaps the most romantic and hottest mini dance club in town. It is also connected to the Kolibri, a quieter cocktail bar next door.

Mariannenstraße 26A, 10999 Berlin
www.facebook.com/dashotel.berlin

NATHANJA & HEINRICH

NEUKÖLLN'S POPULAR IN-LOCATION

Once a secret insider, today Neukölln's popular in-location, Nathanja & Heinrich is located in the so-called Weichselkiez and is always brimming with people. The signature feature of this bar is lots of wood, Art Deco furniture and plants inside. Large windows open onto either side of a street corner and during the day Nathanja & Heinrich is a wonderful place to make use of the Wi-Fi while enjoying a cake and coffee. At night, natural beers on tap are served as well as a decent wine selection. One of the popular drinks is Mezcal Negroni Lost at Sea.

Weichselstraße 44, 12045 Berlin
www.nathanja-heinrich.de

TiER

A NEW WORLD OF DRINKS

Located in the Weserstrasse Neukölln, the living-room bar TiER is known for high-quality cocktails, and for its elegance and modern style combined with the typical Berliner nonchalance. The owner is also famous, although no one has ever seen him. He calls himself "Herr von Tier". Those who think they can spy through the bar windows after midnight are deluded. Herr von Tier makes sure that his world is only seen upon entering the door and until midnight. Taking pictures is strictly forbidden. A large selection of rum and whiskeys, classic long drinks like Old Fashioned or a potent Mescal Sour compete with the experimental creations of TiER. Due to the long opening hours, visitors are welcome to enjoy all drinks on the menu. Indeed, Herr von Tier likes it when guests turn the night into the day.

Weserstr. 42, 12045 Berlin
www.tier.bar

TRUFFLE PIG

BERLIN'S MOST HIDDEN BAR

This is a slightly hidden bar in Berlin's Neukölln district. To get there, one has to follow the pig tracks through Kauz & Kiebitz, press the fire alarm bell and then walk through a secret large mirror before being welcomed to this square marble bar. Velvet chairs radiate cosiness and the cocktail menu is rather playful. Coconut cognac, banana liqueur and the "The Wood, the Bad, the Ugly", based on bourbon that was macerated with woodruff, are substantial. A popular summer cocktail is the "Artists Special", but traditional cocktails and drinks like Martinis can also be enjoyed here. The interior was designed by Studio Karhard, which is highly in demand, especially in Berlin.

Reuterstraße 47, 12047 Berlin

www.trufflepigberlin.de

VELVET

BAR OF THE YEAR

In this bar, they spin and never stir. Once a simple students' bar, Velvet now proudly carries the title "Bar of the Year 2019". Sarah Fischer, Ruben Neideck and Filip Kaszubski are the culinary team at the Velvet Bar in Neukölln. The essences, syrups and concentrates for the cocktails are blanched, fermented, filtered, centrifuged or evaporated. In addition to high-proof alcohol, only seasonal vegetables and fruits from the region are used in the cocktails; wild herbs are often foraged by the bartenders themselves in and around Berlin. A signature cocktail? Every week Velvet offers new creations, however, if a guest likes to drink a classic cocktail, it will be made provided all the ingredients are available. Welcome to Berlin's taste laboratory.

Ganghoferstraße 1, 12043 Berlin
www.instagram.com/velvet.berlin

LERCHEN & EULEN

WARM & FRIENDLY

Night owl or early bird? No problem, gins and coffees can be ordered from dusk until dawn and vice versa at Lerchen & Eulen. Close to Markthalle 9, Lerchen & Eulen is homely, jovial and warm, even in Berlin's bitter-cold winter. Daylight shines through the large windows, and in summer, tables and chairs are placed outside for everyone to absorb every ray of light. The interior reminds one of a 1970s living community where corduroy chairs and sofas in bright colours invite all of the creatures of the dawn and night. Although the brick walls are exposed, Lerchen & Eulen still radiates a warm welcoming flair, with fresh flower bouquets in rustic watering cans brightening up the corners. This bar is also known for its extremely friendly staff.

Pücklerstraße 33, 10997 Berlin
www.lerchenundeulen.de

SHOP

THE STORE X BERLIN

EXCEPTIONAL CONCEPT STORE

The Soho House Berlin wouldn't be the Soho House without The Store. Two floors of fashion, furniture, music, art, and books alongside food from Cecconi's, an Italian restaurant characterised by urban zeitgeist and elegance, The Store Kitchen offers a special shopping experience.

The Store invites the exploration of this innovative take on the retail experience, one that brings local and international creatives together in an ever-evolving conversation. This is a place to feel comfortable and at home in a very elegant way. Exhibitions and events are also part of The Store. And if this is not enough: The Store X Berlin is also available for private hire, receptions and shoots.

Torstraße 1, 10119 Berlin
www.thestores.com/berlin

LUNETTES

MOST BEAUTIFUL EYEWEAR BOUTIQUE

This is probably Berlin's most beautiful eyewear boutique/ store. Located in Mitte, Prenzlauer Berg and Charlottenburg, Lunettes has eyewear for every taste, whether one is looking for unusual vintage sunglasses, or for the most beautiful reading specs from a specific decade. For a precise fit and optimal visuality, Lunettes also offers a customised eye exam service on-site with traditional optical measurement tools. Prescription lenses are crafted from high-quality Zeiss glass. Fine designer frames from Italy, France, Belgium, and England, as well as the in-house line, Lunettes Kollektion, are carefully produced using traditional methods. Originating in Berlin, Lunettes eyewear can be found all over the world, from New York's Soho to Tokyo's Shibuya to Barcelona's Passeig de Gracia.

Bleibtreustraße 29/30, 10707 Berlin
www.lunettes-selection.de

MAXIMILIAN MOGG

TIMELESS MENSWEAR

Men in well-cut suits are rarely seen on Berlin's streets. Maximilian Mogg wants to change this. The aim: timeless menswear. Fit and proportions come first, then everything else. Mogg strives for an individual style, independent of fashion trends. Located in Charlottenburg, the shop is decorated like a living room. Walls in pale green and a striped sofa at the front. The back, painted in terracotta red, allows customers privacy to try on their new pieces. Several racks of suits adorn the walls. Mogg honed his craft with famous London tailors like Edward Sexton and is an advocate of good old-fashioned, early 20th-century sartorial ingenuity. Mogg believes in building a sustainable men's wardrobe made up exclusively of high-quality and timeless pieces.

Bleibtreustraße 27, 10707 Berlin
www.maximilianmogg.de

PAPER & TEA

TEMPLE OF TEA

The large wall gains a completely different meaning in this tea shop. At 7 metres long, this wall stores the world's finest teas, organised library-style from white over green and yellow to Oolong and black teas up to Pu Erh and the country of origin. A separate shelf displays "herbals", namely herbal and healing teas. The store's sleek interiors are clean, yet extend a warm-hearted invitation to a self-determined discovery of the world of fine tea. Besides herbs and leaves, versatile crockery with an Asian touch can be bought as well as traditional and modern tea accessories made from glass, stone, wood, porcelain or metal.

Alte Schönhauser Str. 50, 10119 Berlin
www.paperandtea.de

ANDREAS MURKUDIS

OUTSTANDING CHOICE OF PRODUCTS

Space is the greatest luxury for Andreas Murkudis. Only with sufficient space can things fully unfold. While managing the "Museum der Dinge", Andreas Murkudis established himself in the Berlin art scene. Since the opening of the first shop in 2003, Murkudis creates rooms that invite one to linger, slow down and breathe. The rooms are in contrast to the everyday fast pace and here objects are made in an individual way. Friends, fans and customers are regularly invited to special events to promote dialogue through new impulses. The chosen goal of Andreas Murkudis is to inspire visitors again and again with a diverse selection of special art objects.

Potsdamer Straße 81, 10785 Berlin
www.andreasmurkudis.com

VOO STORE

CREATIVELY DRIVEN CONCEPT SPACE

This concept store is located in the heart of Kreuzberg, occupying a charming 300- square-metre courtyard space on the ground floor of a former locksmith. A careful selection of local and international fashion labels, books, magazines, and art showcase the Berliner lifestyle. All products are displayed in an urban and industrial space. The Voo Store is an enthusiastic advocate for longevity. Everything offered in the shop should become a possession for life, offering design and quality as opposed to short-lived trends. With Voo's in-house cafe – Companion Coffee – the shop serves a variety of speciality coffee, handsourced tea from its personal micro-farms as well as a selection of freshly-baked goods.

Oranienstraße 24, 10999 Berlin
www.vooberlin.com

APTM

LIVING GALLERY FOR DESIGN, ART & CUISINE

This is one of Berlin's most unique locations. Founder and curator Chris Glass transformed a bland factory floor into a living gallery for design, art and cuisine. Set in a hidden courtyard in Wedding, everything from an intimate private dinner to a large presentation can be hosted. aptm is also a place to meet and to shop. The store is glamorous and cool at the same time, huge and yet very intimate, sweet (in pink and light grey) and elegant. Design products from all over the world can be found here such as hanging baskets by Atelier Haussmann, vintage furniture and design articles by Elisa Strozyk or Joa Herrenknecht, carpets, bags, beauty products by Red Flower, and ceramics by Jonathan Adler.

Lindowerstraße 18, 13347 Berlin
www.aptm.berlin

MINIMUM AT AUFBAU HAUS

FURNITURE DESIGN CLASSICS

For more than 20 years, minimum has been shaping Berlin's lifestyle within a multitude of work and living spaces with furniture design classics and new discoveries from Berlin and Europe. In addition to new design favourites and projects by contemporary designers seen in minimum's Berlin stores at stilwerk and Mitte, the shop at Aufbau Haus in Kreuzberg mainly presents new perspectives on Scandinavian work-style and lifestyle, but is also inspired by Germany and other countries. Living collages featuring Muuto, Müller Möbelwerkstätten, HAY, USM, and Nils Holger Moormann inspire dream homes with colourful impulses and serene elements. Other sights: micro-living and new work ideas as well as much more furniture to fall in love with.

Prinzenstraße 85, 10969 Berlin
www.minimum.de/stores/kreuzberg

THE CORNER BERLIN

LUXURY FASHION BOUTIQUES

This concept store is one of the most luxury fashion boutiques in Berlin and the flagship store is located in the heart of Berlin at the Gendarmenmarkt. Everything here is large: high windows, higher walls, and columns. The 750 square metres appear even more expansive shining in glossy white than they already are. The room is open and bright. No pushing and no jostling. The Corner Berlin has a fine range of desirable products – an exciting mix of fashion, perfumes, books, and accessories from luxury labels and newcomer designers from all over the world. Exclusiveness and value are high priority here. Katie Holmes, Suzie Menkes or Claudia Schiffer have already bought at The Corner Berlin. It comes as no surprise: after all, one can shop for glamour.

Französische Straße 40, 10117 Berlin
www.thecornerberlin.de

DO YOU READ ME?!

INTERNATIONAL CONTEMPORARY BOOKS

This is not a standard book shop. This is a reader's heaven. Based in Mitte, do you read me?! offers a curated selection of magazines and books from across the world, covering topics from art, fashion, photography, design and architecture to literature, music, society and contemporary culture. The focus here lies on real, tangible reading items and as it is easy to get lost in all the beautiful publications, one needs to have time to spend in this book store. But no need to panic if in a hurry, do you read me?! ships worldwide and has a fantastic online store as well.

Auguststraße 28, 10117 Berlin
www.doyoureadme.de

EXPLORE

In the explore category you'll find personally selected galleries and art museums to ensure you get your culture fix in Berlin – a treasure trove for cultured travellers. And if you would like to extend your stay with a trip outside Berlin, we have included some of our favourite places to relax.

THE BOROS COLLECTION

IN A CONVERTED BUNKER

The Boros Collection is a private collection of contemporary art located in Mitte. It comprises groups of works by international artists from 1990 to the present day. In a converted bunker, sections of the collection are shown to the public in changing presentations. The Boros Collection shows newly acquired and space-specific works in conjunction with works from the 1990s and 2000s. The presentation of the collection is accessible to the public only in the form of guided tours. For safety reasons, the bunker can only be visited in small groups. There are 1.5-hour guided tours from Thursday to Sunday. The tours take place every half-hour and are conducted in English and German.

Reinhardtstraße 20, 10117 Berlin
www.sammlung-boros.de

KÖNIG GALERIE

CONTEMPORARY ART GALLERY

Founded by Johann König in 2002, this gallery currently represents 40 international emerging and established artists, mostly from a younger generation. König focuses on interdisciplinary, concept-oriented and space-based approaches in a variety of media. This includes showcasing sculptures, videos, sounds, paintings, printmaking, photography and performances. Located in the heart of Kreuzberg, the gallery is surrounded by other museums, popular stores and restaurants. It has successfully placed works in a variety of private and public collections, including the Museum of Modern Art in New York and the Guggenheim Foundation. The artists represented have solo exhibitions with institutions worldwide and regularly partake in prestigious group exhibitions, such as Documenta and the biennials in Venice, Berlin, New York and others.

Alexandrinenstraße 118-121, 10969 Berlin
www.koeniggalerie.com

C/O BERLIN

VISUAL MEDIA AND PHOTOGRAPHY

Whoever is looking for an exhibition house focusing on visual media and photography should visit C/O Berlin. In the heritage-protected America House, located in Charlottenburg, changing exhibitions by international photographers are shown and supplemented by artist talks, lectures, workshops, seminars and tours. C/O Berlin presents internationally known artists and also promotes young talents. C/O Berlin is a charitable foundation and the exhibits are not for sale.

Hardenbergstraße 22-24, 10623 Berlin
www.co-berlin.org

DAS SCHWARZE HAUS

SURROUNDED BY NATURE

This black house is a free-standing house in the middle of the Uckermark. The lower floor is completely made of glass and fits 11 people. Berlin architect Thomas Kröger created a feeling of being surrounded by nature inside the house. Even in the bathtub.

Some consider this house a barn, but the windows are too big for that. Inside, it is predominantly black, thus the owners chose the name "The Black House". The interior is puristic and focuses on the essentials: the landscape. Forests, lakes and rolling hills spread as far as the eye can see. This is the reason why the Uckermark is also called Tuscany of the North.

Pinnow 26A, 17268 Gerswalde
www.dasschwarzehaus.de

GUT WOLLETZ

PICTURESQUE HOLIDAY IDYLL

If you are looking for a charming spot with a great atmosphere for your next holiday, Gut Wolletz is the right place for you. Its immediate proximity to a lake and forests makes this lovingly restored sheepfold a picturesque holiday idyll. Located in the middle of the Schorfheide-Chorin biosphere reserve, GutWolletz is the starting point for a variety of cycling tours, hikes and boat trips. Each apartment comes with its own private terrace, and can accommodate two to four guests. Not far from the Gut Wolletz is the swimming area. As an additional service, a canoe and rowboat can be arranged.

Zur Kastanienallee 12A, 16278 Angermünde
www.gutwolletz.de

STRANDWOOD

HOLIDAY HOUSE WITH SEA VIEW

Welcome to the Island of Rügen. A typical feature of this island are simple boathouses on the shores of the Baltic. Formerly, these houses were intended for the storage and maintenance of ships and fishing gear.

Strandwood stands for an exclusive location directly on the water and for the dominating element of the holiday home: wood. This house is perfectly inserted into an idyllic harbor setting. It captivates through the wood façade, which has been transfigured by wind and weather, and a light-flooded interior design in the style of Scandinavian minimalism. Natural building materials and clear structures create clarity and space. All rooms receive light from two sides and thanks to the wood-burning stove and the sauna a cozy atmosphere is created all year round.

Am Hafen 2, 18586 Gager
www.strandwood.de

COPYRIGHT

The publisher would like to thank the following for their kind permission to reproduce their photographs:

Erin Wulfsohn (@erinwulfsohn) for Pursch Artistes (@purschartistes) p.7, picture from Hanni Heinrich; Angel Santos p. 10; Gorki Apartments p. 14; Giacomo Morelli - Gorki Apartements p. 16; Mark Seelen, Soho House Berlin p. 18, 20; SO/ Berlin Das Stue p. 22, 24; Amo by Amano p. 26, 28; Hotel Zoo Berlin p. 30, 32; Sir Savigny p. 34; Hotel Michelberger p.36; Philipp Obkircher p. 38; Provocateur Hotel p. 40-43; Panama, Philipp Langenheim & Corina Schadendorf p. 104; Robert Rieger p. 112-115; White Kitchen Berlin p. 116; Juni Fotografen p. 118-120; Staffan Sundström p. 138-141; Lunettes p. 184; aptm p. 194; minimum, Yves Sucksdorff p. 196; The Corner Berlin p. 198; Installationsansicht mit Arbeiten von Michel Majerus, Foto: Boros Collection, Berlin © NOSHE p. 204; Jose Dávila, The Moment of Suspension, 2019/20, Courtesy the artist & KÖNIG GALERIE, Photo by Roman März p. 206; David von Becker p. 208; Das schwarze Haus p. 210-213; Robert Wunsch p. 214; Edzard Piltz p. 216-219.

BERLIN

CAPE TOWN

MILAN

PALMA DE MALLORCA

PARIS

REYKJAVÍK

STOCKHOLM

TBILISI

AND MORE AVAILABLE AT

www.travelcolours.guide